A Guide to AMERICAN STATES

Delaware

THE FIRST STATE

MEDIA ENHANCED BOOKS
AV2 BY WEIGL
ADDED VALUE • AUDIO VISUAL

www.av2books.com

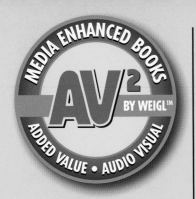

AV² provides enriched content that supplements and complements this book. Weigl's AV² books strive to create inspired learning and engage young minds in a total learning experience.

Your AV² Media Enhanced books come alive with...

Audio
Listen to sections of the book read aloud.

Key Words
Study vocabulary, and complete a matching word activity.

Video
Watch informative video clips.

Quizzes
Test your knowledge.

Go to **www.av2books.com,** and enter this book's unique code.

Embedded Weblinks
Gain additional information for research.

Slide Show
View images and captions, and prepare a presentation.

BOOK CODE

L 7 7 6 9 4

AV² by Weigl brings you media enhanced books that support active learning.

Try This!
Complete activities and hands-on experiments.

... and much, much more!

Published by AV² by Weigl
350 5th Avenue, 59th Floor
New York, NY 10118
Website: www.av2books.com   www.weigl.com

Library of Congress Cataloging-in-Publication Data

Winans, Jay D.
 Delaware / Jay D. Winans.
     p. cm. -- (A guide to American states)
 Includes index.
 ISBN 978-1-61690-780-8 (hardcover : alk. paper) -- ISBN 978-1-61690-455-5 (online)
 1. Delaware--Juvenile literature. I. Title.
 F164.3.W565 2011
 975.1--dc23
                         2011018319

Printed in the United States of America in North Mankato, Minnesota

052011
WEP180511

Project Coordinator Jordan McGill
Art Director Terry Paulhus

Photo Credits
Every reasonable effort has been made to trace ownership and to obtain permission to reprint copyright material. The publishers would be pleased to have any errors or omissions brought to their attention so that they may be corrected in subsequent printings.

Weigl acknowledges Getty Images as its primary image supplier for this title.

Contents

The Harbor of Refuge Light is 76 feet tall and stands at the mouth of Delaware Bay.

Introduction

Located on the eastern seaboard, Delaware had the honor of being the first state to **ratify** the U.S. Constitution, earning it the nickname the First State. Two Delawareans, John Dickinson and George Read, helped write the Constitution, which was **unanimously** approved by a Delaware state convention on December 7, 1787.

While exploring the coastline north of Virginia in 1610, Captain Samuel Argall found refuge during a storm in a bay that he named in honor of the governor at Jamestown. The governor's name was Sir Thomas West, baron de la Warr. Eventually, the bay, the river that flowed into it, the entire coastal area, and even the American Indians who lived there came to be known as Delaware.

Since the 1990s, Wilmington's riverfront area has enjoyed an economic revival.

NASCAR racing at Dover International Speedway features Jimmie Johnson and other top drivers.

Delaware was ruled by several different countries before it became a state. In 1638, Sweden established a permanent colony at Fort Christina, in the same location as present-day Wilmington. New Sweden prospered and found a lasting peace with the local American Indians, but the colony failed to grow because it was not supported by Sweden. In 1655, New Sweden was taken over by the Dutch and absorbed into their New Netherlands colony. The Dutch, in turn, were conquered by the English in 1664, and the three counties of Delaware became part of the land given in 1682 to William Penn, founder of Pennsylvania. Delaware was governed from Philadelphia until the American Revolution.

Delaware declared itself separate from Britain and Pennsylvania on June 15, 1776. Each year, Delaware residents celebrate the second Saturday in June as Separation Day.

Where Is Delaware?

Delaware lies on the Delmarva Peninsula, which it shares with Maryland and part of Virginia. Delaware borders Pennsylvania to the north and Maryland to the south and west. Most of the state's eastern boundary is shaped by Delaware Bay. New Jersey is located on the other side of the bay. The state's southeastern boundary is the Atlantic Ocean.

More than 80,000 vehicles each day cross the Delaware Memorial Bridge, which links New Castle, Delaware, with Pennsville, New Jersey.

The Delaware Memorial Bridge crosses the Delaware River and connects northern Delaware with New Jersey. Southern Delaware is linked to New Jersey by the Cape May–Lewes Ferry, which crosses Delaware Bay. Major highways, including I-95, I-295, and I-495, pass through the most populated section of the state, which is the city of Wilmington and its surrounding area in the extreme north. Wilmington is a short drive from numerous major cities, including Philadelphia, Baltimore, New York, and Washington, D.C.

Because the state is small, many companies in Delaware must do business with partners in nearby states, including Pennsylvania, Maryland, New Jersey, and New York. Wilmington is one of several eastern cities that form a densely populated industrial region. The cities in this region, which stretches from Baltimore, Maryland, to Boston, Massachusetts, are an important part of the national economy.

The Cape May–Lewes Ferry can hold up to 1,000 passengers and 100 cars.

I DIDN'T KNOW THAT!

Delaware's flag shows the state coat of arms in the center of a diamond upon a field of colonial blue. Thomas Jefferson declared Delaware a "jewel among the states," which may be why one of its nicknames is the Diamond State. Delaware is also known as the Blue Hen State and Small Wonder.

Many of the companies that are headquartered in Delaware do the majority of their business outside the state.

The official state mineral is sillimanite.

Delaware's official state beverage is milk. In 2009, peach pie became the official state dessert.

Colonial blue and buff are the official state colors. The colors represent those of General George Washington's uniform.

During the Civil War, 12,284 Delawareans fought for the Union. Of these soldiers, 954 were African Americans.

Philadelphia International Airport is the closest major airport to Wilmington. The airport is about a 25-minute drive from the city.

Mapping Delaware

Occupying less than 2,500 square miles, Delaware is the second-smallest state in the country. Only Rhode Island is smaller. The land area of Delaware covers 1,954 square miles, or about 78 percent of the total. The state's remaining area consists of water. With Delaware Bay to the east and the Atlantic Ocean to the southeast, the state has more than 380 miles of shoreline.

Sites and Symbols

STATE SEAL
Delaware

STATE WILDLIFE ANIMAL
Gray Fox

STATE FLOWER
Peach Blossom

DECEMBER 7, 1787

STATE FLAG
Delaware

STATE MARINE ANIMAL
Horseshoe Crab

STATE TREE
American Holly

Nickname The First State

Motto Liberty and Independence

Song "Our Delaware," words by George B. Hynson and Donn Devine, music by Will M. S. Brown

Entered the Union December 7, 1787, as the 1st state

Capital Dover

Population (2010 Census) 897,934

Ranked 45th state

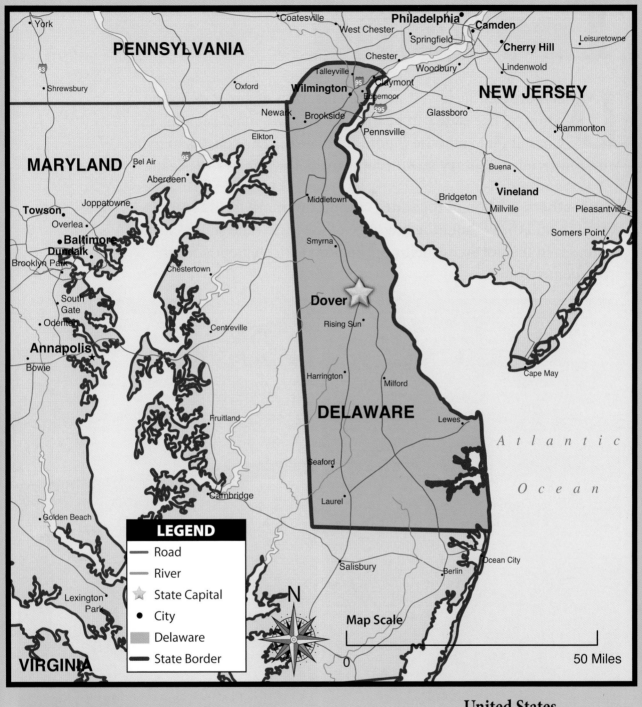

PENNSYLVANIA

York
Coatesville
West Chester
Philadelphia
Camden
Springfield
Cherry Hill
Leisuretowne
Chester
Shrewsbury
Oxford
Talleyville
Woodbury
Lindenwold
Wilmington
Claymont
Edgemoor
NEW JERSEY
Newark
Brookside
Pennsville
Glassboro
Hammonton
Elkton
MARYLAND
Bel Air
Buena
Aberdeen
Middletown
Bridgeton
Vineland
Joppatowne
Millville
Pleasantville
Towson
Overlea
Smyrna
Somers Point
Baltimore
Dundalk
Brooklyn Park
Chestertown
Dover
South Gate
Rising Sun
Odenton
Centreville
Harrington
Milford
Annapolis
Bowie
DELAWARE
Lewes
Atlantic
Fruitland
Ocean
Golden Beach
Seaford
Cambridge
Laurel
Cape May

LEGEND

— Road
— River
⭐ State Capital
• City
▨ Delaware
— State Border

N

Map Scale

0   50 Miles

Salisbury
Berlin
Ocean City

Lexington Park

VIRGINIA

STATE CAPITAL

Dover became the capital of Delaware in 1777. The city, the second largest in Delaware, has a population of about 37,000. Many people who live in Dover work for the state government.

United States

Hawai'i   Alaska

Delaware

The Land

Delaware has the lowest average **elevation** of any state in the country. The state can be divided into two main regions, the Coastal Plain and the Piedmont Plateau. The coast is marshy with numerous **tributary** streams and rivers flowing to the ocean.

The southern portion of the state is sandy, but more fertile soil can be found inland throughout the majority of the state. The state's elevation increases in the northern Piedmont region, which extends south from Pennsylvania.

BRANDYWINE RIVER

The Brandywine River, also known as Brandywine Creek, flows from southeastern Pennsylvania into northern Delaware before emptying into the Christina River.

SANDY SHORES

From the mouth of Delaware Bay to the Maryland border, Delaware has more than 24 miles of sandy beaches along the Atlantic Ocean.

SWEET GOLDENROD

Delaware chose sweet goldenrod as the official state herb in 1996.

CHRISTINA RIVER

Wilmington developed in the region where the Christina River flows into the Delaware River.

I DIDN'T KNOW THAT!

In 1889 a huge storm off the coast of Delaware destroyed 40 ships and killed 70 people.

The Christina River is a tributary of the Delaware River, and the Brandywine River is a tributary of the Christina River.

The town of Delmar straddles the border between Delaware and Maryland. Its motto is "The Little Town Too Big for One State."

The boundary between Delaware and Maryland is the Mason-Dixon Line. This line is named for the British surveyors Charles Mason and Jeremiah Dixon.

The average elevation in Delaware is approximately 60 feet. Ebright Road is the highest point in the state at only 448 feet, while the lowest point is sea level at the Atlantic coastline.

Summer sun and surf bring crowds to Rehoboth Beach.

Climate

Delaware's climate is similar to that of other Middle Atlantic states. The summers are warm and humid, with an average July temperature of 75° Fahrenheit. Winters in the state are cool, and average temperatures are a mild 35°F. The average yearly precipitation in Delaware is 45 inches.

The town of Millsboro boasts the highest and lowest temperatures officially recorded in Delaware. The town hit a summer high of 110°F in 1930 and a winter low of –17°F in 1893. Although hurricanes rarely hit Delaware directly, rain and winds from tropical storms are a common summer occurrence.

Average Annual Temperatures Across Delaware

There is not a great deal of variation in the average annual temperatures recorded at different cities and towns in Delaware. What factors might account for the similarity?

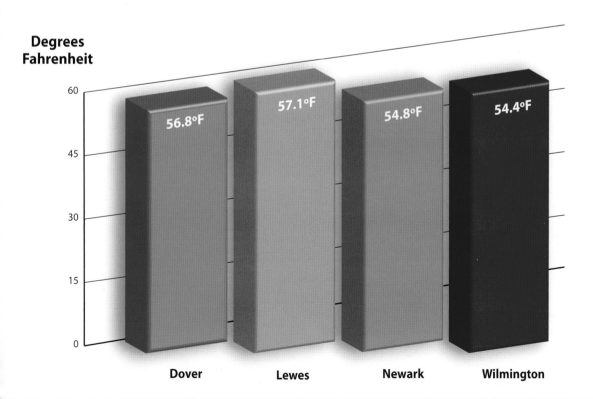

Degrees Fahrenheit

Dover	56.8°F
Lewes	57.1°F
Newark	54.8°F
Wilmington	54.4°F

July through September marks the peak growing and eating season for Delaware watermelons.

Natural Resources

Mineral resources in Delaware are not numerous and make up only a small part of the state's economy. The state sits on a foundation of gravel and sand and offers very little in the way of resources for mining operations. In fact, Delaware usually ranks last in the nation in the value of mineral production. All three counties in Delaware produce sand and gravel. The state is also a source for Brandywine blue granite, a building stone used for decoration.

The level landscape, moderate coastal climate, and reasonably fertile soil provide Delaware farmers with the means to raise crops. The money earned from crops accounts for about one-fifth of the state's farm income. Soybeans and corn are the most valuable crops. Barley, potatoes, watermelons, and wheat are also grown in the state.

Delaware farmers plant and harvest about 1,600 acres of potatoes annually. The crop has a value of up to $5 million or more.

Plants

About one-third of Delaware is covered by forests. Common trees in the state include beech, hickory, holly, oak, and sweet gum. Wildflowers flourish in the state's swamps and marshes. Round ponds called Carolina bays are the only places where certain rare species of plants survive.

The Cypress Swamp that straddles the Delaware and Maryland border in the south is the most northern location of the bald cypress. Azaleas, magnolias, pink and white hibiscus, and violets are a colorful part of the state's landscape.

CYPRESS TREES

Cypress trees can grow up to 120 feet tall and live as long as 600 years.

AMERICAN HOLLY

Delaware made the American holly its official state tree in 1939.

FLOWERING MAGNOLIA

Magnolia trees are so popular in Delaware that the state even has a town named Magnolia after the trees that bloom there.

VIOLETS

Hundreds of species of flowers, including several types of violet, grow wild in Delaware.

Animals

Delaware's Atlantic shore attracts seabirds and other coastal wildlife to the salt marshes. Wetlands cover nearly 30 percent of the state. These areas are a crucial habitat for Delaware's coastal wildlife. In 1963 the federal government established the Prime Hook National Wildlife Refuge to protect the birds of the wetlands.

Delaware's animal population can be found in fields, rivers, and forests throughout the state. Beavers, deer, foxes, minks, muskrats, otters, rabbits, and raccoons all live in Delaware.

There are more than 200 species of bird in the state. The wetlands of Delaware Bay attract huge numbers of migrating waterfowl to the western shore. Snow geese, Canada geese, and other migrating birds spend the winter months in Delaware. The state's lakes and ponds contain many kinds of fish, including bass, carp, eel, and trout. Delaware's coastal waters are home to clams, crabs, oysters, and sea trout.

EGRETS

Great egrets usually feed in shallow rivers, streams, and marshes and make their nests in nearby trees and shrubs.

TIGER SWALLOWTAIL

The state butterfly, the tiger swallowtail, has a wingspan of 3 to 5 inches. Swallowtails like to feed on nectar from pink or red flowers.

HORSESHOE CRABS

In springtime, horseshoe crabs emerge from shallow ocean waters to spawn on Delaware beaches. Each female may deposit up to 20,000 eggs at a time.

WHITE-TAILED DEER

A recent survey counted more than 3,600 white-tailed deer in Delaware.

Tourism

Delaware's beaches are the most popular tourist and outdoor destinations in the state, drawing 6 million visitors each year. Nearly 25 miles of sandy Atlantic beaches extend from the tip of Delaware Bay to the Maryland border. Many of these beach areas are located in state parks.

The Historic Houses of Odessa, in New Castle County, provide visitors with an insight into life in the 1700s and 1800s. Strolling down the quiet streets, tourists can visit the Corbit-Sharp House, which is listed on the National Register of Historic Places. The house contains examples of beautiful furniture made by local cabinetmakers.

One last stop in Delaware should be the Johnson Victrola Museum. The museum is a tribute to Eldridge Reeves Johnson, from Wilmington. Johnson helped invent the **gramophone** and founded the Victor Talking Machine Company, which later became RCA Victor. Johnson also improved the quality of vinyl records by applying electric currents to wax.

NASCAR

Rapid-fire pit stops are part of the fun when the NASCAR Sprint Cup series competition comes to Dover International Speedway.

ZWAANENDAEL MUSEUM

The Zwaanendael Museum, at Lewes, recalls the history of the short-lived colony founded by the Dutch in 1631.

REHOBOTH BEACH RESORT

The Rehoboth Beach resort area offers amusement parks, arcades, summer programs, go-carts, and water slides along with plenty of sun and sand.

JOHNSON VICTROLA MUSEUM

Delaware had an important role in the development of the earliest record players, many of which are displayed at the Johnson Victrola Museum in Dover.

Industry

At the beginning of the 1800s, Eleuthère Irénée du Pont de Nemours, who immigrated from France to Delaware, began operating a gunpowder factory on a property near the Brandywine River. The DuPont factory produced gunpowder for the U.S. government during the War of 1812, the Mexican-American War, and the Civil War. In peacetime the explosive power of gunpowder was used to clear obstructions during building projects, such as the transcontinental railroads and the Panama Canal.

Industries in Delaware
Value of Goods and Services in Millions of Dollars

The finance, insurance, and real estate industry is the largest one in Delaware. Why have so many banks and other finance companies chosen to locate their headquarters in the state?

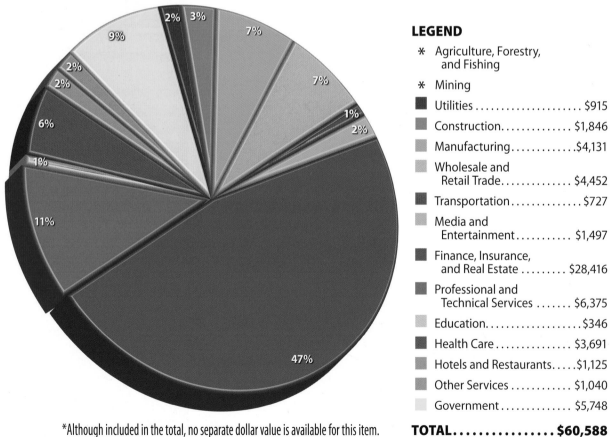

LEGEND

* Agriculture, Forestry, and Fishing
* Mining
- Utilities $915
- Construction. $1,846
- Manufacturing. $4,131
- Wholesale and Retail Trade. $4,452
- Transportation. $727
- Media and Entertainment. $1,497
- Finance, Insurance, and Real Estate $28,416
- Professional and Technical Services $6,375
- Education. $346
- Health Care $3,691
- Hotels and Restaurants. $1,125
- Other Services $1,040
- Government $5,748

TOTAL. $60,588

*Although included in the total, no separate dollar value is available for this item. Percentages may not add to 100 because of rounding.

During the Civil War, DuPont powder mills supplied gunpowder for the Union side.

In the 1900s the DuPont company developed its business beyond the manufacturing of gunpowder and began to produce materials, such as nylon, that were based on modern chemistry. Today, DuPont is one of the largest companies in the United States, with a value of more than $35 billion.

Delaware is a major producer of chemicals and special materials made from chemicals. It is also home to other manufacturing and processing industries. These include automobile assembly plants, oil refineries, packaging plants, and food-processing plants.

The engineers who built the First Transcontinental Railroad, linking the eastern and western United States, used Delaware-made gunpowder to blast through and around mountains.

Goods and Services

The sale of goods is an important part of Delaware's economy. In the state's earliest days, the sale of agricultural products provided the majority of its income. In the 1700s, Delaware's flour mills were renowned. In fact, the price for wheat was set in Wilmington.

Paper and cotton mills were established in Brandywine Village toward the end of the 1700s. As the **Industrial Revolution** gave rise to automation, factories began to play a greater role in Delaware's economy.

The U.S. broiler chicken industry began in Delaware in 1923. Today, the industry employs more than 20,000 people throughout the country.

Companies such as DuPont, Hercules, and ICI Americas are responsible for producing a majority of the chemicals, dyes, and powders that make Delaware the Chemical Capital of the World. These companies produce pigments, petrochemicals, rubber, synthetic fibers, and plastics that are used all over the world.

Since the early 1900s, Delaware laws have encouraged businesses to establish their headquarters in Delaware. In the 1980s, large banks began to move to Delaware to take advantage of the reduced taxes on financial institutions.

Delaware is known for its **broiler chickens**. The broiler-chicken business accounts for more than two-thirds of Delaware's farm income and is one of the state's largest enterprises. Yearly sales of broiler chickens earn the state more than $700 million.

Sussex County, the number-one broiler-chicken-producing county in the United States, calls itself the birthplace of the broiler industry. It produces more than 200 million broiler chickens a year, nearly twice as many as the second-ranked U.S. county, in Alabama. The majority of the grain grown in Delaware is used to feed chickens.

I DIDN'T KNOW THAT!

In the mid-1780s, Oliver Evans built the country's first completely automatic flour mill. He built the mill on Red Clay Creek, near his hometown of Newport.

Wallace Carothers invented the synthetic fiber known as nylon in the 1930s while he was employed at DuPont.

Many credit card companies have operations in Wilmington.

Fisher's Popcorn, a regional company with a store on Fenwick Island, is famous for its caramel corn.

There is no sales tax in the state of Delaware.

Building railroad cars was a major industry in Delaware during the 1800s.

For nearly 100 years, beginning in 1863, the Jackson and Sharp Company of Wilmington built railroad cars, trolleys, and ships that were used throughout the world.

American Indians

When Europeans arrived in what is now the state of Delaware, American Indians were already living there. The Europeans called these people by the name Delaware. The Indians called themselves the Lenape, or the Lenni Lenape, which means "original people." They lived along the Atlantic seaboard from the area of Cape Henlopen in Delaware to Long Island in New York.

Some of the Lenape lived in large villages of 200 to 300 people, but most lived in smaller groups. Men generally did the hunting, and women did most of the farming, growing corn, squash, and beans. Women were mainly responsible for cooking and child raising. Both men and women took part in music, art, and storytelling.

Lenape children learned how to shoot a bow and arrow, and they competed against each other to sharpen their skills.

At first the Lenape enjoyed a friendly relationship with the Europeans. In 1737, in an event that came to be known as the Walking Purchase, William Penn's sons falsely claimed that the Lenape's ancestors had sold land to the Penns more than 50 years before. According to a false **deed**, the Penns were to receive all the land that could be walked in one and one-half days. The Penns then measured the area using three of their best runners, thus acquiring 1,200 square miles of land. The Lenape complained but eventually submitted to the Penns and moved off the land.

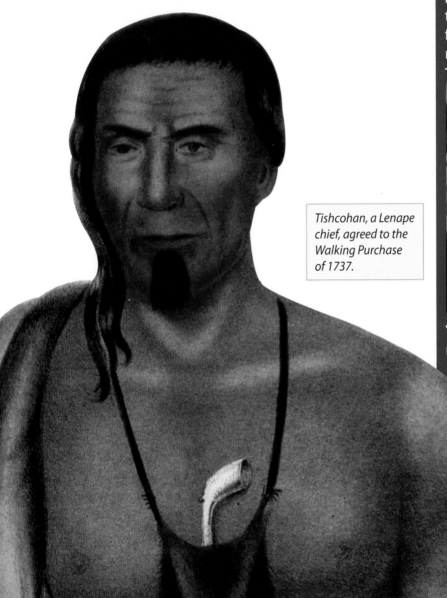

Tishcohan, a Lenape chief, agreed to the Walking Purchase of 1737.

The Lenape play a traditional game called Pahsahëmen, similar to football, in which the men play against the women. The men are permitted only to kick the ball, while the women may throw, kick, or carry the ball.

Between 1600 and 1900, the Lenape were often forced to relocate. Many now live in Oklahoma.

The Nanticoke, who were related to the Lenape, once controlled most of the Delmarva Peninsula.

In the French and Indian War, the Lenape fought against British expansion. Later, they even supported the American Revolution for a time.

Henry Hudson's landing at Delaware Bay in 1609 was painted by Jean Leon Gerome Ferris about 300 years later.

Explorers

T he first European to see Delaware's shores was Henry Hudson in 1609. Hudson was an English explorer employed by the Dutch. At the time, Hudson was searching for the Northwest Passage, a waterway that was rumored to connect the Atlantic and Pacific oceans. On his way to exploring the area around New York Harbor and the Hudson River, Hudson sailed into Delaware Bay and past the mouth of the Delaware River.

In 1610, Captain Samuel Argall named Delaware Bay while exploring the coast north of Virginia. Other notable explorers of Delaware's coastal waters were Cornelius May in 1613 and Cornelius Hendricksen in 1614. Hendricksen traveled up the Delaware River and traded with American Indians in the region.

Timeline of Settlement

Early Exploration and Settlement

1609 Henry Hudson is the first European to enter the body of water now known as Delaware Bay.

1610 Samuel Argall names the bay and river for Sir Thomas West, baron de la Warr, or Delaware.

1614 Cornelius Hendricksen begins trading with the Lenape Indians.

First Colonies Established

1631 The Dutch found the colony of Zwaanendael, near present-day Lewes.

1638 Swedes set up a colony at Fort Christina, now Wilmington.

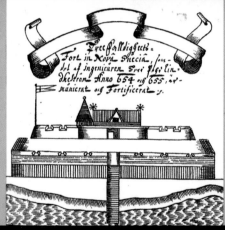

1639 The first black settler, a man named Anthony, arrives in Delaware. He later becomes an assistant to the colonial governor of New Sweden.

Further Settlement and Colonization

1655 The Dutch defeat the Swedes, making Delaware part of New Netherland.

1664 Delaware becomes a British colony after the Dutch are defeated.

1682 Control of the Delaware colony passes to the English Quaker William Penn.

Statehood and Civil War

1787 On December 7, Delaware becomes the first state to ratify the U.S. Constitution.

1861–1865 Although a slaveholding state, Delaware sides with the Union during the Civil War.

Early Settlers

T he first European settlers arrived in the Delaware area in 1631, only 11 years after the Pilgrims landed at Plymouth. A small group of settlers sailed from Holland in the ship *De Walvis* under the command of Captain Peter Heyes. When they arrived in North America they founded a settlement near what is now the Lewes and Rehoboth Canal. They named the settlement Zwaanendael, which means "the valley of the swans."

Map of Settlements and Resources in Early Delaware

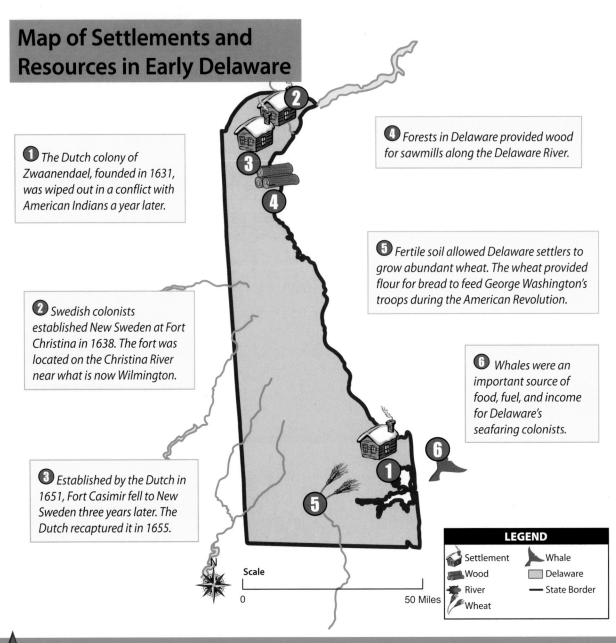

1 The Dutch colony of Zwaanendael, founded in 1631, was wiped out in a conflict with American Indians a year later.

2 Swedish colonists established New Sweden at Fort Christina in 1638. The fort was located on the Christina River near what is now Wilmington.

3 Established by the Dutch in 1651, Fort Casimir fell to New Sweden three years later. The Dutch recaptured it in 1655.

4 Forests in Delaware provided wood for sawmills along the Delaware River.

5 Fertile soil allowed Delaware settlers to grow abundant wheat. The wheat provided flour for bread to feed George Washington's troops during the American Revolution.

6 Whales were an important source of food, fuel, and income for Delaware's seafaring colonists.

Scale

0   50 Miles

LEGEND

Settlement Whale
Wood Delaware
River — State Border
Wheat

In 1632, de Vries set sail for the colony. When he arrived, he found the camp destroyed. He was told by the American Indians who lived nearby that there had been a battle between the Zwaanendael settlers and some of the Indians. None of the Dutch had survived the conflict.

In 1638, Peter Minuit, a Dutchman and the former governor of New Amsterdam, led a group of Swedish colonists to the area that has become Wilmington. They arrived in the ships *Kalmar Nyckel* and *Vogel Grip* and landed on the shores of the Christina River. There they established the settlement of Fort Christina, named in honor of Sweden's young queen.

In 1654, Johan Rising, the governor of New Sweden, captured Fort Casmir, the Dutch fortification on the north bank of the Delaware River. He was not able to keep the fort for long, as Peter Stuyvesant, the governor of New Amsterdam, recaptured the fort and all of New Sweden in 1655, bringing an end to Swedish colonies in the New World.

Swedish dignitaries in 2003 marked the 365th anniversary of the founding of New Sweden by dancing with Lenape Indians at a ceremony in Wilmington.

Notable People

Although a small state, Delaware has played a big role in American history. A U.S. vice president, a leader of the American Revolution, and one of the nation's foremost makers of historical films have all made their home in Delaware. Scientists living in Delaware have charted the stars and developed life-saving techniques.

LAPPAWINSOE
(1700s)

Lappawinsoe was a Lenape chief at the time of the 1837 agreement known as the Walking Purchase. This agreement allowed the sons of William Penn to claim—based on a false deed—about 1,200 square miles of Indian land. Lappawinsoe and other Lenape Indians were unhappy about the agreement, but they eventually had no choice but to move off the land.

CAESAR RODNEY
(1728–1784)

Born on a farm in Kent County, Caesar Rodney grew up to become one of Delaware's foremost political and military leaders. He signed the Declaration of Independence, served in the Continental Congress, and helped to defend Delaware during the American Revolution. He held office as Delaware's chief executive from 1778 to 1781.

ANNIE JUMP CANNON
(1863–1941)

The daughter of a Delaware shipbuilder, Annie Jump Cannon grew up in Dover. She developed a way to classify stars based on their temperature and appearance. She assigned the letters O B A F G K M to different groups of stars. Generations of astronomers learned her system by using this phrase: Oh! Be a Fine Girl. Kiss Me!

JOE BIDEN
(1942–)

Born in Pennsylvania, Joe Biden moved with his family to Delaware in 1953. He was only 29 years old when he won election to his first Senate term in 1972. In 2008, Barack Obama picked Biden to run for vice president. In November of that year, voters throughout the country elected Obama as president and Biden as vice president.

KEN BURNS
(1953–)

Ken Burns spent much of his boyhood in Newark. He makes films and television programs about history. His works include *The Civil War*, a prize-winning series on public television. The Delaware Historical Society named Burns the winner of its Delaware History Makers Award for 2011.

I DIDN'T KNOW THAT!

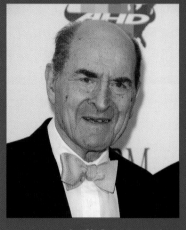

Henry Heimlich (1920–), a surgeon and inventor, was born in Wilmington. He developed the Heimlich maneuver, which is used to stop people from choking.

Randy White (1953–), one of the most honored defensive linemen in pro football history, played high school football in Wilmington. He led the Dallas Cowboys to a Super Bowl championship in 1978 and joined the Pro Football Hall of Fame in 1994.

Population

Delaware is one of the most densely populated states in the country. Of the 897,934 people living in Delaware in 2010, many made their homes in the urban and industrial centers in the northern part of the state. The average **population density** in the state was about 460 people per square mile of land area. Only six other states and the District of Columbia ranked higher than Delaware in population density in 2010.

Delaware Population 1950–2010

The graph shows that the population of Delaware more than doubled between 1960 and 2010. What does that indicate about the change in Delaware's population density during the same period?

Number of People

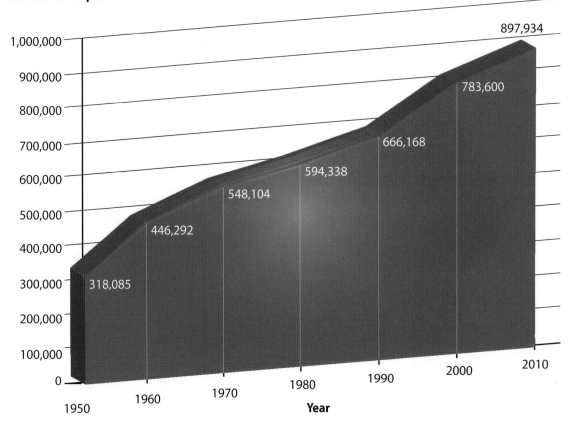

Year	Population
1950	318,085
1960	446,292
1970	548,104
1980	594,338
1990	666,168
2000	783,600
2010	897,934

More than 73 percent of Delaware's people are of European descent. Another 21 percent are African American, and 3 percent are Asian American. Fewer than 1 percent are American Indians. Hispanics, who may be of any race, account for more than 7 percent of the population.

Between 2000 and 2010, Delaware experienced higher than average population growth compared to the rest of the United States. The population of Delaware grew by nearly 15 percent, whereas the national population grew by less than 10 percent.

Workers in Dover, Delaware's second-largest city, sewed the spacesuits worn by U.S. Apollo astronauts on voyages to the Moon.

Politics and Government

The state of Delaware has had four constitutions. The state adopted its current constitution in 1897. According to the state constitution, the governor serves as the head of the executive branch for a four-year term and may be reelected only once. Other members of the executive branch include the lieutenant governor, attorney general, insurance commissioner, and treasurer.

In the same election in November 2008, Joe Biden won the U.S. vice presidency and a seventh term as U.S. senator from Delaware. He gave up his Senate seat to become the nation's 47th vice president.

Born into one of Delaware's most influential families, Pete du Pont worked as a lawyer for the DuPont company before serving as governor of Delaware from 1977 to 1985.

The General Assembly, or legislature, is the state's lawmaking branch of government. The legislature consists of two chambers. The Senate has 21 senators, and the House of Representatives has 41 members.

All Delaware judges must be nominated by the governor and then confirmed by the Senate. The state's judicial branch is made up of several courts. The highest court is the state Supreme Court. There are also superior courts, courts of chancery, family courts, common pleas courts, and justice of the peace courts.

Delaware's state song is called "Our Delaware."

Here is an excerpt from the song:

*From New Castle's rolling meadows,
Through the fair rich fields of Kent,
To the Sussex shores hear echoes,
Of the pledge we now present;*

*Liberty and Independence,
We will guard with loyal care,
And hold fast to freedom's presence,
In our home state Delaware.*

The state seal of Delaware was adopted on January 17, 1777.

Delaware has three electoral votes in U.S. presidential elections. The state is represented in the national government by two senators and one member of the House of Representatives.

Cultural Groups

As founders of one of the first settlements in Delaware, the Swedish have left a rich heritage in the state. The Holy Trinity Church, often called Old Swedes Church, is the nation's oldest church still in operation. It was built in Wilmington in 1698 by descendants of the first Swedish settlers. Each December the church celebrates the traditional Swedish Festival of Light in honor of Sankta Lucia. An important figure in Swedish tradition, Sankta Lucia carries the message of Christmas, coming with light in her hair on the darkest morning of the year. She is a symbol of compassion, love, and light.

Delaware's African American population grew in the mid-1900s as African Americans migrated from the South to the industrialized North. More than 10,000 people turn out each year for Positively Dover, a festival that celebrates the state's rich African American heritage.

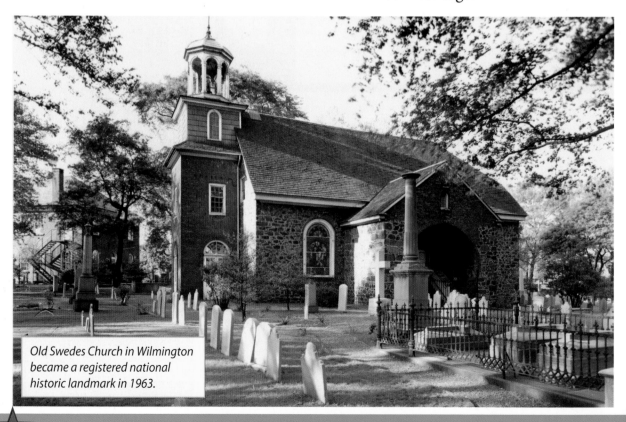

Old Swedes Church in Wilmington became a registered national historic landmark in 1963.

Instead of modern farm machinery, many Amish still use horses and mules to harvest their crops.

Cheswold, in Kent County, has a small community of Nanticoke Indians. In 1979 the Nanticoke held their first powwow since the 1940s. Today the Nanticoke Indian Powwow is among the largest traditional powwows on the east coast. This celebration of dance and culture attracts visitors from across the country.

Amish farms and settlements dot the landscape around the outskirts of Dover in Kent County. The Amish are members of a traditional farming society that avoids contact with the modern world. Amish beliefs restrict the use of modern technology, including automobiles and electricity. The Amish make all their own clothing as well as colorful quilts, which can be bought at roadside stands.

Richard Allen purchased his freedom and became a minister while living in the Dover area.

I DIDN'T KNOW THAT!

Barratt's Chapel, in Frederica, is considered the cradle of Methodism in the United States. In 1784 the chapel was the site of a historic meeting that led to the founding of the Methodist Episcopal Church.

Richard Allen, a slave in Delaware during his youth, became the founder of the African Methodist Episcopal Church.

Cultural festivals in Delaware include the Greek Festival in Wilmington, the German Saengerbund Oktoberfest in Newark, and the Hispanic Festival in Millsboro.

In the 1800s a group of Polish potato farmers from Long Island settled in Kent.

Little Italy, a neighborhood in Wilmington, is home to the annual St. Anthony's Italian Festival, which takes place in June.

The Nanticoke Indian Museum, in Millsboro, opened in 1984. It is the only American Indian museum in Delaware and contains artifacts that are more than 10,000 years old.

Amish traditions call for travel by horse and buggy rather than by automobile.

Arts and Entertainment

Perhaps Delaware's most important contribution to the history of art is the work of Howard Pyle. Born in 1853 in Wilmington, Pyle is known for the realism and the historical detail of his illustrations. Hailed as the founder of modern American illustration, Pyle taught and influenced countless young illustrators, including Maxfield Parrish and N. C. Wyeth. These artists are known as the Brandywine School after the school that Pyle founded in Wilmington in about 1900.

Felix Darley was another great illustrator of the 1800s. He spent the last 29 years of his life in Claymount, where he produced many of his best known illustrations. Darley's fame and popularity arose from his illustrations for the novels of great writers such as Charles Dickens, Nathaniel Hawthorne, and Edgar Allan Poe.

Decades after his death, Howard Pyle's works still hold a prominent place in many American museums.

The Delaware Art Museum was started in 1912 by a group of Wilmington **patrons** who wished to put many of Howard Pyle's artworks on display. Since that time, the museum has built a permanent collection of American illustrations, with a special emphasis on Pyle's work. The museum also owns works by Edward Hopper, Frederic Edwin Church, Deborah Butterfield, and John Sloan, as well as the most important U.S. collection of art by the **Pre-Raphaelites**.

Founded in 1999, the Wilmington Ballet Company develops and trains young dancers. Ballet performances have featured internationally known guest artists. OperaDelaware is Wilmington's opera company. It began staging operas in 1945. OperaDelaware performances take place at the Grand Opera House and are accompanied by a live orchestra. In addition to performing world premieres and family operas, the company also provides educational, community, and regional outreach programs.

Actress Yvette Freeman is the daughter of jazz pianist Charles Freeman. She was born in Wilmington and graduated from the University of Delaware. Freeman had a long-running role in the medical series ER.

Sports

A small state such as Delaware does not have a large enough population to attract a major professional sports team. Instead, Delaware's enthusiastic sports fans have the opportunity to enjoy a variety of community and college-level sports.

The Wilmington Blue Rocks play Class-A minor-league baseball at Frawley Stadium. The team is **affiliated** with the Kansas City Royals, a Major League Baseball team. Also popular are the Delaware Bobcats, a women's ice hockey club. The Bobcats have been playing since 1975.

Many Delaware sports fans follow the Fightin' Blue Hens of the University of Delaware at Newark. The university's sports program includes baseball, basketball, football, field hockey, golf, lacrosse, rowing, soccer, softball, tennis, swimming, and track and field. Some activities are available for both women and men, others only for women or only for men.

Golf is a popular form of recreation in Delaware. More than 20 courses statewide belong to the Delaware State Golf Association. Baywood Greens and Bear Trap Dunes Golf Club are two championship courses located in the state.

Delaware Park, in Wilmington, offers more than 100 days of Thoroughbred horse racing every year. The park is also one of the few U.S. tracks to feature racing by purebred Arabian horses.

Champion figure skater Kimmie Meissner does most of her training at the University of Delaware in Newark.

Sport fishing is hugely popular in Delaware. An annual weakfish contest includes prizes for the largest weakfish caught. Another popular contest is the Delaware Sport Fishing Tournament, which lasts throughout the year. Contestants compete in a variety of saltwater and freshwater categories, including bluefish, marlin, swordfish, and trout.

Both residents and visitors enjoy hiking in Delaware's great outdoors. The state has more than 80 miles of trails that wind through 10 state parks. Avid hikers can take the Trail Challenge, which involves hiking 15 state-park trails within a period of one year. Winners receive the Expert Hiker Award.

National Averages Comparison

T he United States is a federal republic, consisting of fifty states and the District of Columbia. Alaska and Hawai'i are the only non-contiguous, or non-touching, states in the nation. Today, the United States of America is the third-largest country in the world in population. The United States Census Bureau takes a census, or count of all the people, every ten years. It also regularly collects other kinds of data about the population and the economy. How does Delaware compare to the national average?

Comparison Chart

United States 2010 Census Data *	USA	Delaware
Admission to Union	NA	December 7, 1787
Land Area (in square miles)	3,537,438.44	1,953.56
Population Total	308,745,538	897,934
Population Density (people per square mile)	87.28	459.64
Population Percentage Change (April 1, 2000, to April 1, 2010)	9.7%	14.6%
White Persons (percent)	72.4%	68.9%
Black Persons (percent)	12.6%	21.4%
American Indian and Alaska Native Persons (percent)	0.9%	0.5%
Asian Persons (percent)	4.8%	3.2%
Native Hawaiian and Other Pacific Islander Persons (percent)	0.2%	—
Some Other Race (percent)	6.2%	3.4%
Persons Reporting Two or More Races (percent)	2.9%	2.7%
Persons of Hispanic or Latino Origin (percent)	16.3%	8.2%
Not of Hispanic or Latino Origin (percent)	83.7%	91.8%
Median Household Income	$52,029	$58,380
Percentage of People Age 25 or Over Who Have Graduated from High School	80.4%	82.6%

*All figures are based on the 2010 United States Census, with the exception of the last two items. Percentages may not add to 100 because of rounding.

How to Improve My Community

Strong communities make strong states. Think about what features are important in your community. What do you value? Education? Health? Forests? Safety? Beautiful spaces? Government works to help citizens create ideal living conditions that are fair to all by providing services in communities. Consider what changes you could make in your community. How would they improve your state as a whole? Using this concept web as a guide, write a report that outlines the features you think are most important in your community and what improvements could be made. A strong state needs strong communities.

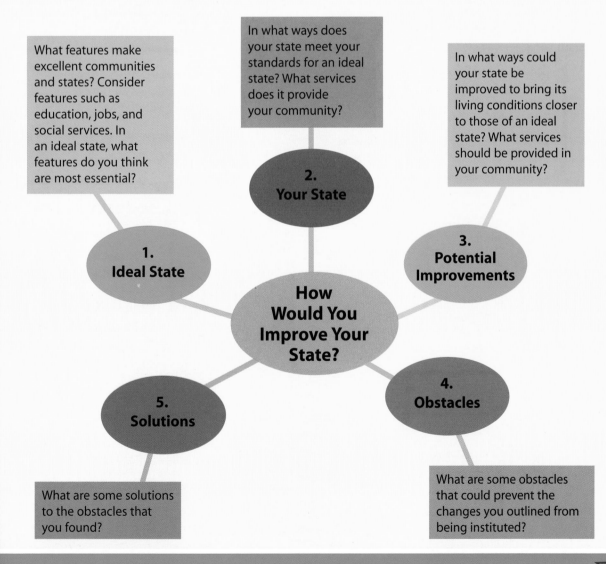

What features make excellent communities and states? Consider features such as education, jobs, and social services. In an ideal state, what features do you think are most essential?

In what ways does your state meet your standards for an ideal state? What services does it provide your community?

In what ways could your state be improved to bring its living conditions closer to those of an ideal state? What services should be provided in your community?

2. Your State

1. Ideal State

3. Potential Improvements

How Would You Improve Your State?

5. Solutions

4. Obstacles

What are some solutions to the obstacles that you found?

What are some obstacles that could prevent the changes you outlined from being instituted?

Exercise Your Mind!

Think about these questions and then use your research skills to find the answers and learn more fascinating facts about Delaware. A teacher, librarian, or parent may be able to help you locate the best sources to use in your research.

1 Which colonial patriot is shown riding a horse on the U.S. quarter issued for Delaware in 1999?

a) John Dickinson
b) Caesar Rodney
c) George Read

2 Settlers from which country landed at The Rocks?

a) Sweden
b) Finland
c) Norway
d) Denmark

3 Delaware's state seal depicts a sheaf of wheat, an ear of corn, and what?

a) a weakfish
b) a ladybug
c) a peach tree
d) an ox

4 True or False: The smallest county in Delaware contains the largest population.

5 The battleship USS *Delaware* was **commissioned** in what year?

a) 1710
b) 1810
c) 1910
d) 2001

6 True or False: Delaware was used as a lookout post for German submarines during World War II.

7 How tall is Delaware's highest sand dune?

a) 20 feet
b) 80 feet
c) 150 feet
d) 420 feet

8 Who was known as the Penman of the Revolution?

Words to Know

affiliated: connected with

broiler chickens: young chickens raised for meat rather than eggs

commissioned: brought into active service

deed: a sealed contract, usually relating to property

elevation: height above sea level

endangered species: a kind of animal or plant that is in danger of completely dying out

freedman: a person who has been freed from slavery

gramophone: an early record player

Industrial Revolution: the widespread replacement of manual labor by machines in the late 1700s, which began in Great Britain and spread to the United States and other countries

patrons: wealthy people who support the arts

peat: natural material found in damp and marshy regions, often cut and dried for use as a fuel

population density: the average number of people per unit of area

Pre-Raphaelites: a group of British painters and writers in the mid-1800s who took inspiration from art made before Raphael, an Italian painter of the 1500s

ratify: approve

tributary: a stream that flows into another stream or river

unanimously: agreed by everyone

Index

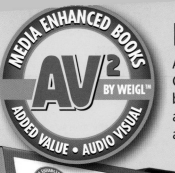
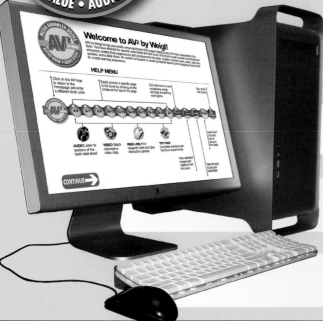